WALLLESS SPACE

WAVE BOOKS / SEATTLE AND NEW YORK

ERNST MEISTER
WALLESS SPACE

///

TRANSLATED BY GRAHAM FOUST AND SAMUEL FREDERICK

PUBLISHED BY WAVE BOOKS

WWW.WAVEPOETRY.COM

WANDLOSER RAUM COPYRIGHT © 1979 RIMBAUD
VERLAGSGESELLSCHAFT MBH, AACHEN, GERMANY
ENGLISH TRANSLATION AND INTRODUCTION
COPYRIGHT © 2014 BY GRAHAM FOUST AND SAMUEL FREDERICK
ALL RIGHTS RESERVED

WAVE BOOKS TITLES ARE DISTRIBUTED TO THE TRADE BY
CONSORTIUM BOOK SALES AND DISTRIBUTION
PHONE: 800-283-3572 / SAN 631-760X

LIBRARY OF CONGRESS CATALOGING-IN-PUBLICATION DATA
MEISTER, ERNST, 1911–1979.
[WANDLOSER RAUM. ENGLISH]
WALLLESS SPACE / ERNST MEISTER ; TRANSLATED BY
GRAHAM FOUST AND SAMUEL FREDERICK. — FIRST EDITION
PAGES CM.
ISBN 978-1-933517-95-7 (LIMITED EDITION HARDCOVER)
ISBN 978-1-933517-94-0 (TRADE PBK.)
I. FOUST, GRAHAM W., 1970– II. FREDERICK, SAMUEL. III. TITLE.
PT2625.E3224W313 2014
831'.914—DC23
2013041220

DESIGNED AND COMPOSED BY QUEMADURA
PRINTED IN THE UNITED STATES OF AMERICA

9 8 7 6 5 4 3 2 1

FIRST EDITION

INTRODUCTION

Ernst Meister is one of the great but neglected lyric poets of postwar Germany, a writer who remained on the margins and steadfastly refused to conform to the prevailing trends of his time. Rejecting the aesthetics and politics of both the Gruppe 47 and the 68er-Bewegung, Meister practiced a nonprogrammatic experimentalism—that is, one altogether unlike that of the Wiener Gruppe or the concrete poets. He therefore remained largely a poet's poet, despite being admired by a few prominent and sometimes controversial literary figures (among them Peter Handke and E. M. Cioran) and being awarded the prestigious Georg Büchner Prize. (For a more comprehensive biography, see our introduction to *In Time's Rift*, our translation of *Im Zeitspalt*, published by Wave Books in 2012.)

As is the case with the bulk of Meister's late work, the poems in *Wandloser Raum* (*Wallless Space*), the poet's final collection—published in 1979, the year of his death—combine rigorous and at times arcane philosophical thought with sparse, fractured, and highly allusive language. At the same time, however, they make frequent reference to quotidian objects (a jug, an hourglass, a chair) and domestic spaces, though these are not meant to offer comfort. Instead, living spaces turn over into the abstract realm of existence, the things that populate these spaces serving as reminders of their (and our) groundlessness—the absence of being that, for Meister, threatens to engulf us all. In one poem from the present volume, "Es haben sich," Meister's language conveys both senses of this abyss in the word *das Grundlose*, which means not only that which is without a ground, but also that which is without a reason. These are poems that resist this apparently pointless nothingness even as they explore it, and in doing so allow access to the metaphysical spaces opened up in and through the often trivial things of this world. Meister's great achievement, we believe, is his celebration of language's power as both product of and protection against the existential void. For example, in this collection's first poem Meister begins by apostrophizing not any muse, but the paper on which he writes:

> You sustaining
> four, you
> corners of region!

The four corners of the everyday piece of paper double as the corners of a more expansive region, one given eschatological resonance by means of an allusion to the book of Revelation ("I saw four angels standing on the four corners of the earth, holding the four winds of the earth"). Poetry emerges from the ability of the lyrical I to endure these winds ("I stand / between air"), and the page in front of him provides him with the necessary (if temporary) support.

Guided by our belief that each book Meister produced in

his last decade is a unified work that is also a part of a larger nexus, our leading principle in translating this late verse has been to render these volumes as individual collections while also maintaining the poet's concentrated linguistic arsenal as deployed across publications. With the help of the new critical edition of his poetry (*Gedichte: Textkritische und kommentierte Ausgabe*, published by Wallstein Verlag in late 2011) we have been able to achieve a detailed understanding of Meister's careful diction and to follow particular motifs through various drafts and stages so as to render as precisely as possible the numerous references, images, and concepts that cycle through the poems.

We have thus attempted to match Meister's diction whenever possible with a consistent English equivalent. For example, in variations on "nothing" (*Nichts, Nichtigkeit, nicht,* etc.), one of Meister's central concerns, consistency is especially important, and we have tried to ensure that these echoes are just as plain in English as they are in the German and that each variation on the word matches a similar variation in our rendering. Meister's more subtle repetitions can be equally important, such as with the root *entsetz-*, which appears as the present participle *entsetzend* in *In Time's Rift* and as the adverb *entsetzlich* in *Wallless Space*. We match the two by favoring one of the many possible meanings for both occurrences, translating the former with the present progressive "shocking," so as to hint at the verb's secondary meaning of "displacing," and the latter with the adverb "shockingly."

With slight variations on the same root, we have been similarly careful, even though "perfect" matches are not always possible—or even desirable. With forms of the words *kreisen* (to circle) and *kreiseln* (to spin or spiral), for instance, which Meister uses in two poems in this volume, such a match might have produced precision, but at the expense of losing Meister's careful linguistic play. Strict consistency in diction would turn the phrase "Es kreist / das Kreiselnde," from this book's second poem, into the rather bland "Spinning itself / circles around." We felt the echo of the repeated *kreis-* was more important than any such faithful rendering, choosing therefore to imitate this doubled sound with a recurring "spin-," while capturing the specific "circling" that *kreisen* denotes with the additional adverb "round": "Spinning itself / spins round." While the appearance of *kreisen* in a later poem demands the more precise "to circle," we still insist on linking these two uses of the verb by repeating this adverb: "circle round."

In translating these volumes in their entireties, we have also sought to correct what we feel are flawed or weak approaches on the part of previous translators, though of course we also acknowledge that their work has at times been useful to us. One such example (from page 88 of this volume) can be found in Jean Boase-Beier's rendering of the poem that begins "Geist zu sein," which presents a challenge to any translator in the participle *aufgehoben*, a word with a range of often contradictory meanings, including "abolished," "canceled out," "contained," "preserved," and "saved up":

Was ist, ist

und ist aufgehoben
im wandlosen Gefäß
des Raums.

"What is," for Meister—and by this he means existence—
is "contained" and therefore "saved up" and "preserved" in
the "vessel" of space. Except that this vessel is no vessel at
all: it has no walls or boundaries. Like the titular "rift in time"
of Meister's previous volume of poetry, it designates an in-
finite space that does not so much "preserve" us as over-
whelm us, turning our existence—and existence as such—
into something frighteningly insignificant, and easily elimi-
nated. "What is," therefore, is also *lost* in this infinite space,
"abolished" or "canceled out" precisely because it is, paradox-
ically, "contained" by the void, the abyss of being.

Boase-Beier's translation makes use of line breaks to
heighten the English-language reader's experience of this
section of the poem:

What is is

and is not
held in the wall-less vessel
of space.

While this is a compelling solution to the problem at hand, it
fails to address the multifaceted nature of the word that Meis-

ter has chosen by dividing it too cleanly into opposites that have no shared value, thereby eliding the initial verb ("what is *is*"), which in this rendering is made to serve as the passive auxiliary for "held." Our goal was to retain the exact structure of Meister's lines, while also finding an expression that makes palpable the simultaneous but contradictory processes described by "aufgehoben." Although English does not have a word that contains the varied and opposed meanings that this verb does, there do exist anagrammatic English near-equivalents, the words "bottled" and "blotted," each of which suggests the other's opposite meaning. Our solution:

> What is *is*
>
> and is bottled up, blotted out
> in the wallless vessel
> of space.

Because Meister is concerned with expressing the impossible process of "containment" in a void via a verb that at once affirms, negates, and finally makes evident these processes' inextricability—they are, after all, unified in a single German word—our use of anagrams seems to us closer to his interests than does Boase-Beier's enjambment. Moreover, our translation captures the German word's enactment of the Hegelian dialectic (undoubtedly of great importance to Meister, who was well versed in continental philosophy), as these adjacent opposites—each of which *contains* the other—become partly reconciled in their shared sounds.

Meister's work makes frequent use of the language of other philosophers as well. The words of Friedrich Nietzsche, for instance (on whose work Meister began, but did not complete, a doctoral dissertation), can be found in a number of poems in *Wallless Space*. See, for example, the poem that begins "Immer noch," in which, as Meister scholar Stephanie Jordans has pointed out, "the crooked truth" echoes the dwarf's assertion in *Thus Spake Zarathustra*: "Everything straight lies . . . All truth is crooked." But it is Martin Heidegger, more than any other thinker, who haunts the poems in this book. The philosopher's famous discussion of the jug in his essay on "The Thing," in particular, resonates in the lines (quoted above) from which Meister takes the volume's title: "The empty space, this nothing of the jug, is what the jug is as the holding vessel." Heidegger's terminology is furthermore evident in these poems' repeated variations on "being" (*sein, Nichtsein, Dasein, Seiendes*) as well as in one unusual usage of *Wesen* (essence) as a verb:

> Hier in dem Punkt,
> der sieht,
> wie du stehst,
>
> west alle Zeit.

Here at this point,
which sees
how you stand,

all time unfolds.

In his late work, Heidegger frequently used this archaic verb,
in part because it allowed him to emphasize that being is not
an entity but is rather that which makes *being* at all possible
—it is the groundless ground that appears (and disappears) in
a kind of ceaseless *essencing*. *Wesen* provides him with an im-
portantly intransitive alternative to *sein* (to be). In modern
German the verb is no longer used, but it can be found in de-
rivative verbs such as *verwesen* (to decay), also a favorite word
of Meister's. We have opted to translate *wesen* with the En-
glish verb "to unfold," which some translators of Heidegger
have also used, and which captures the processual nature of
being while also suggesting its essential concealment and un-
concealment.

The new critical edition of Meister's poems has addition-
ally allowed us to avoid potential missteps where—as is often
the case—Meister's syntax is highly ambiguous. Take, for in-
stance, the opening lines of the poem quoted earlier:

Wo das Kreuz ist
der Sanduhr,
wurzelt der Blitz.

Initially, this three-line sentence seems disrupted by the odd placement of the verb in the first line—the basic content of the sentence would appear to be, "Where the cross of the hourglass is, lightning takes root." But annotations to the poem in the recent critical edition make clear that Meister is thinking of a specific passage in Heidegger's lectures on Nietzsche—he in fact sent an early version of this poem, along with a brief letter, to Heidegger in 1961—and that Meister has, in his copy of the lectures, actually penciled a cross next to Nietzsche's hourglass image:

> ". . . The eternal hourglass of existence is turned upside down again and again, and you with it, speck of dust!"

Given this bit of marginalia, we felt the lines must be rendered with the unusual syntax intact, thus maintaining Meister's elliptical expression so that the possessive referent of the "hourglass" is lost between the lines—

> Where the cross is
> of the hourglass,
> lightning takes root.

—lost, as the image would have it, in time.

GRAHAM FOUST AND SAMUEL FREDERICK

I

Ihr haltsamen
vier, ihr
Ecken der Gegend!

Ich steh
zwischen Luft,
den Atem sinnend,

indes, mir übers Haupt,
der Raum sich hebt
mit unzähligen Himmeln.

You sustaining
four, you
corners of region!

I stand
between air,
pondering my breath,

while up and over my head
space lifts itself
with innumerable heavens.

Die Diener tot
des Hauses. Im Saale
schwebt die Speise.
Alles kreiselt, die Schindeln
sträubt das Dach.

Auf Sessellehne steht,
den Hals gereckt,
ein Hahn, Skelett
im stummen Krähn.

Es kreist
das Kreiselnde.
Du mit, der aus
den Fenstern blickt
des Hauses.

The servants dead
of the house. Supper
hovers in the hall.
Everything spins, the roof
gets its shingles up.

Standing on a chairback,
its neck stretched,
a rooster—skeleton
silently crowing.

Spinning itself
spins round.
As do you, looking
out the windows
of the house.

Ein falscher
Klang in der Luft
und ein falsches
Auge im Licht,

daß die Vögel
über dem See
im Fluge stolpern,

die Beute
den Schnäbeln
entfällt

und dem Jäger,
im Rohr versteckt,
die Haare
zu Berge stehn.

A false
note in the air
and a false
eye in the light,

so that the birds
over the lake
falter in their flight;

their prey
falls out of
their beaks;

and the hairs
of the hunter,
hidden in the stalks,
stand on end.

Wo das Kreuz ist
der Sanduhr,
wurzelt der Blitz.

Hier in dem Punkt,
der sieht,
wie du stehst,

west alle Zeit.

In ihm
wärest du
immer geboren,

und nicht
mit Scham
möchtest du sein.

Where the cross is
of the hourglass,
lightning takes root.

Here at this point,
which sees
how you stand,

all time unfolds.

At it
you would be
forever born,

and you'd
like to be
without shame.

Was sich da selbst
beschreibt im
wachen Traum,

das aus Wasser,
Erde, Luft, Feuer
(so sagten die Alten):

die vier, eine
Kunst miteinander,

deren Regent ist die Lust,
deren Regent ist das Ach.

That which describes
itself there
in waking dream,

made of water,
earth, air, fire
(so said the ancients):

the four, an
art with one another,

whose regent is the sense of pleasure,
whose regent is the sound of lament.

Immer noch
laß ich mich glauben,
es gebe
ein Recht des Gewölbes,
die krumme Wahrheit
des Raums.

Vom Auge gebogen,
Unendlichkeit,
himmlisch,
sie biegt das Eisen,
den Willen, sterblich
ein Gott zu sein.

To this day
I let myself believe
there may be
a law to the curved vault,
the crooked truth
of space.

Bent by the eye,
infinity,
empyreal,
it bends the iron,
the will to be
a god, mortally.

Dort auf den Klippen
ein Gemurmel, scheint dir,
vom Nicht und Nichts.

In deiner Nähe
die Welle schlägt an.

Da! aus
gebreitetem Meer
springt hoch auf
ein Delphin.

Over on the cliffs
a muttering, it seems to you,
of Not and Nothingness.

Somewhere near you
the wave crashes in.

There! out of
the spread-out sea
leaps up high
a dolphin.

... auf dessen Kopf
ein Schatten liegt
und auf dem Schatten
ein Stein
und auf dem Stein
ein Schatten—

. . . on whose head
lies a shadow
and on that shadow
a stone
and on that stone
a shadow—

Es haben sich
die großen Vögel
am Himmel versammelt.

Der Älteste schreit.
Sie kreisen.
Der Kreisel hält sie.

Die Hälse gestreckt,
zischen Scharen
ins Grundlose.

The giant birds
have assembled
in the sky.

The oldest shrieks.
They circle round.
The spinning holds them.

Necks outstretched,
the whole gaggle plummets
into groundlessness.

Du stirbst in
Zufall oder Muße.
Die Erde, die Heimat,
verbirgt den
Stummen für lange,

der Worte gemacht hat,
von Tönen weiblich verführt
und Farben einer Pflanzung
im Leeren.

(Du wolltest doch
Augen noch haben
und Ohren beim
Sternuntergang.)

You die in
contingency or leisure.
Earth, the homeland,
a long time hides
the voiceless one,

who made words,
womanly seduced by sounds
and colors of a bower
in the emptiness.

(And yet you still
wanted to have eyes
and ears at
the stars' demise.)

Der großen namenlosen
Vögel grausiges
Gelächter.

Sie rauben dir,
die Oberen, was du
kindisch hältst.

Umsonst und kränkelnd
zwischen Auf- und Untergang
die Sehnsuchtssonne.

The great and nameless
birds' gruesome
guffaws.

They rob you,
those above, of what you
cling to, childishly.

Ailing and in vain
between rising and setting—
the pining sun.

Der von den Sonnen,

Himmelshäuptern,

gesponnene Faden,

der wahrhaft schwarze,

durch unsere Leiber gezogen—

wir in den Zeiten

Aufgereihte . . .

That which by those suns,
heads of heaven,
is spun, the thread,
the truly black one,
strung through our bodies—
we who are aligned
all through time . . .

Sie tragen die Eimer
hinauf, hinunter,
sie füllend mit Blut
und Wasser der Wesen,
sie leerend in Gossen,
wo Gassen nicht sind.

Spiel ruhig mit Worten.
Das raten sie dir, die
listigen Töchter, sie,
jenseits von Zeugung,
die vogelgestimmten.

They carry the buckets
on up, on down,
filling them with blood
and the water of beings,
emptying them into drains
where no lanes exist.

Go ahead and toy with words.
This they advise you, these
cunning daughters, they,
beyond procreation,
the bird-voiced ones.

Es gibt
im Nirgendblau
ein Spiel, es heißt
Verwesung.

Es hängt
am Winterbaum
ein Blatt, es
dreht und
wendet sich.

Ein Schmetterling
ruht aus
auf Todes
lockerer Wimper.

In blue
nowhere there's
a game known as
decay.

Turning
and swiveling,
one leaf is
hanging
from winter's tree.

A butterfly
rests itself
on death's
loose eyelash.

Die alte Sonne
rührt sich nicht
von der Stelle.

Wir
in dem
dämmrigen Umschwung

leben
die Furcht oder
die schwere Freude.

Liebe—
Verlaß und
Verlassen,

von ihr
haben wir gewußt
auf dem Trabanten,

eh alles
vorbei.

The old sun
does not move
from its spot.

We
in this
twilit turnabout

live
dread or
weighty joy.

Love—
depend on it,
abandonment;

we knew
about it
on the satellite

before all was
over.

Gewitter
wandelten über
den See und stießen
ans Fenster mit Donner.
Blitze lasen
unsrer Gesichter Schrift.

Thunderstorms
advanced across
the lake and slammed
against the window, rumbling.
Bolts of lightning read
our faces' script.

Ach, als
ob wir, uns nah,
nicht wüßten
von den ganz entblößten
Wangen, und daß
beinern sei
das Ufer
des hungrigen Meers.

Alas, as if we,
so close to ourselves,
didn't know
of the stripped-away
cheeks, and that
the edge
of the starved sea
was all bone.

Duft der Blumen,
einziger
Gedanke noch.

Ein Steingewicht außer-
dem und ein
Riß wie bei Glas

quer durch
Schädel und Himmel.

Nichts
trennt mich von dir.

Scent of flowers,
only
thought left.

A stoneweight, further-
more, and a
crack as in glass

right smack
across skull and sky.

Nothing
keeps me from you.

Atemlos

so weit zu springen:

in die nächste

Nachbarschaft, die

allernächste zur

letzten

gesprochenen Silbe.

To jump so far,
breathlessly:
into the next
neighborhood, the
one right next to
the last
spoken syllable.

II

Wir leben
von den Entfernungen.

Der Tod
kommt uns vor
so weit wie der höchste
Stern.

Ein Geschäftiges der Natur
setzt Maße in uns.

We live
off the distances.

Death
seems to us
as far as the highest
star.

A busyness in nature
gives us dimension.

Ewigkeit—
fast als Gegenstand
erscheint sie
schlechtem Begreifen.

Sie ist aber
nie, niemals endendes
Fließen und Fliehn.
DENK ES GENAU.

Ob die Zeit
sich verzehre als Zeit,
der Leichnam
fragt es nicht.

Eternity—
it appears
almost as an object
to those slow to grasp.

It is, however,
never, ever ending
flowing and fleeing.
THINK IT EXACT.

Whether time
consumes itself as time,
the corpse
does not ask.

Die Erzählung
von dem, das war,
ist nur enthalten
im Zerfall.

Die Toten nämlich,
unfähig sind sie
der umständlichen
Fabel ihrer selbst.

Dabei
wäre das Grab
gerade der Ort
von Erzählen.

The story
of that which was
is contained only
in ruin.

The dead, namely,
they're incapable of
the circuitous
fable of themselves.

Even though
the grave would be
the very place
of storytelling.

Was Erde sei,
erfahre ich nicht,
wenn ich selbst
Erde bin.

Es ist also Leben
alles, es ist
der Erkenntnis Ton
in den Sphären.

I won't find out
what earth might be
when I myself
am earth.

It's life, then, that's
everything; it's
the sound of understanding
in the spheres.

Die Gestalt, die
Dasein heißt,
hat zum Vater
der Abgründe Abgrund.

Und die Mutter,
sehr glänzend,
heißt Weh,
diesseits und jenseits.

Gerettet sind wir
durch nichts,
und nichts
bleibt für uns.

The figure, the one
called existence,
has as father
the abyss of abysses.

And the mother,
quite radiant,
is here and hereafter
called woe.

We are saved
by nothing,
and nothing
remains for us.

Du Erde voller Schädel,
was sag ich, und was
ist Sagen?

Es macht die Todesrechnung
den Zwang,
das Rechte zu finden.

Das ist seltsam,
und eine Dankbarkeit
gibts.

You Earth full of skulls,
what am I saying, and what
is saying?

The payment that death exacts
demands
the search for what is right.

That is odd,
and therein
is thankfulness.

Lange hast du, scheint es,
gewartet, um ins
Flüchtige zu gelangen,
denn erst jetzt bist du da.

Nun fragst du,
was es war,
das im Augenblick
ist.

It's been a long time, it seems,
that you've waited
to get into what is fleeting,
for only *now* are you there.

Now you ask
what that was,
which *right* now
is.

Da ist kein Schöpfer,

da ist kein Zeuge,

da ist sie selbst

aus sich selbst,

Natur, sie allein—

und ich

wäre einsam

in ihr?

There's nary a Maker,
there's nary a witness,
there's only Nature,
who brings herself
about herself, she alone—
and I'm
supposedly lonely
in her?

Warum erschrecke ich
über Seiendes,
obwohl ich
zu ihm gehöre?

Was ist es
mit dem Unterschied
dessen, das lebt
und das stirbt?

Why am I frightened
by what is,
even though I
belong to it?

What is it
with the difference
between what lives
and what dies?

Das dir zugesagte
Nichtsein wischt
alles Gedachte
weg.

Das Denken krümmt sich
im Wissen darum
und ist doch genötigt,
Welt zu verstehn.

The nonbeing
assured you washes
all that was thought
away.

The mind doubles over
in the knowledge of it
and is still obliged
to understand world.

Gegenwart
voller Geschrei
des Bewußtseins.

Zwar sagen sich
Worte hin,
es ist auch

die Luft beständig,
Kopf und Fuß
sind gehalten.

(Hin und wieder
den Abgrund
versteh ich.)

The present
rife with the clamor
of consciousness.

To be sure,
words can be said;
the air, too,

is constant;
head and foot
are maintained.

(Every now and then
the abyss,
I understand it.)

Gewiß, ich war
ein Same, ich denke
alles von diesem
nicht aus. Erde

werde ich sein, ich
denke sie, in welcher
wachsen die
unwissenden Binsen.

As is known, I was
a seed; I think
all things from out of
this not. Earth

I will be, I
think it, in which
sprout up the
unknowing rushes.

Krumen der Erde, wir,
Sand und Steinen gesellt
unterm bröckelnden Mond,

fern einst,
ungeheuer entbunden
vom Menschsein . . .

Manches
wissen wir, aber
denken es nicht,

denken nicht Zeit.

Humus of Earth, we,
joined with sand and stones
under the disintegrating moon,

once distant,
enormously delivered
from being human . . .

We know
some things, but
do not think them,

do not think time.

»Ein Wort
mit all seinem Grün«,
so las ich.

»Das Nichts mit
all seinem Grün«
ist möglich zu sagen,

denn es weiß
die lebendige Welt
außer uns ja

nichts von sich selbst.——
So denkt euch
und das Andere.

"A word
with all its green,"
I once read.

"Nothingness with
all its green"
is possible to say,

because apart from us
the living world
knows nothing,

of course, of itself—
So think yourselves
and the other.

Wie sehr wir
Gemischte sind!
Du siehst es

auf Märkten,
dabei
totes Tiergesicht.

Du bist
außer dir niemand
und alle doch.

How very
commingled we are!
You see it

at markets,
along with
a dead animal face.

You are
no one but you
and yet everyone.

Nimm die Dinge
als gegeben von seiten
bündiger Natur,

die aus dem,
was sie hat,
Lebendiges zimmert.

O Mensch.

Take things
as given by nature,
aligned and concise,

which constructs
what's living
out of what it has.

O humanity.

(gelesen bei Jean Ziegler)

Wie sie also höchst
unbeholfen, Kinder,
Hungerskelette, riesige,

Spinnen, einander
stützend, hintappten und
krochen zu dem

Stacheldrahtzaun, diesen
zu überwinden. Natürlich,
der fängt sie.

Ich will es behalten.

(read in Jean Ziegler)

The way that they thus
most clumsily, children,
famished skeletons, gigantic,

spiders, supporting
one another, groped about and
crept to the

barbed-wire fence to go
over. Needless to say,
it catches them.

I want to hold on to it.

Unerhört: Da-sein,
zwischen Ewigkeit und Ewigkeit
der fleischliche Traum,
hat er auch Alltag.

Zu erzählen hätte ich
längst von dir,
die mit Wahrheit

knöchern im Boden liegt,
nicht einsam.

Unheard of: Being-here,
between eternity and eternity,
the carnal dream—
there, too, a routine.

I would long ago have
told of you,
who with truth

lies bony in the ground,
not alone.

(zu Montaigne)

Wie es einer
gedacht hat,
Sterben:

Sich drehn
von der Seite der
Erfahrung auf die

der Leere, un-
geängstet, ein
Wechseln der Wange,

nichts weiter.

(on Montaigne)

As someone
once thought it,
dying:

Turning
oneself over from
experience to

emptiness, un-
afraid, a
switching of cheeks,

nothing more.

(zu Valéry)

Weder Tag noch Nacht,
weder Stein noch Stern . . .

Das Äußerste und
das Schwerste ist,

Nicht-da-sein
denken zu müssen.

Wie soll ein Bewußtsein
zu sterben lernen,

sich schicken in seinen
Gegensatz?

(on Valéry)

Neither day nor night,
neither stone nor star . . .

What's most extreme and
most difficult is

having to think
Not-being-here.

How is one consciousness
to learn to die,

to give in to its
opposite?

»Im Tode
des Todes quitt«
(ich spreche es nach),

und da du
Gott losließest
im Dasein schon:

wie entschwert und
reinlich ist
gedachten Ichs Zustand!

"In death
rid of death"
(I'm reciting it),

and as you've
let go of God
in being, here:

how deburdened and
cleanly the
imagined I's condition!

Es ist der Tod
nicht Bruder des Gedankens.

Anders als groß, das
Heimweh zertritt er.

Du, Erde, ein wie
unsäglich Tatsächliches.

Death—it is
not the brother of thought.

Different from huge, it
tramps down homesickness.

You, earth, an as-if-
unspeakable matter-of-factness.

Geist zu sein
oder Staub, es ist
dasselbe im All.

Nichts ist, um
an den Rand zu reichen
der Leere.

Überhaupt
gibt es ihn nicht.
Was ist, ist

und ist aufgehoben
im wandlosen Gefäß
des Raums.

To be spirit
or dust, it's all
the same in the universe.

Nothing is, with
which to reach the edge
of the emptiness.

That edge is
not even there.
What is *is*

and is bottled up, blotted out
in the wallless vessel
of space.

Aber wir sind doch
Kinder der Erde—
wissen wir's nicht?

Zugehörig dem Ursprung,
dürften uns
dessen Bestimmungen

fremd nicht sein.
Doch entsetzlich
aufgespalten scheint

der Anfang der Anfänge selbst.

And yet we are
children of Earth—
don't we know that?

Belonging to the very beginning,
its determinations
should be not

strange to us.
But shockingly
split open seems

the onset of onsets itself.

Tagelöhner
dieser Verzweiflungen—
Hast du
die Erde gewollt?

Du warst diese Erde
im Mutterleib schon.
Nichts als dich einzuholen,
ist dir bestimmt.

Day laborer
of these desperations—
did you
want the earth?

You were this earth
in the womb already.
Nothing but catching up to yourself
is destined you.

Lange Erkenntnis. Dafür
abwesenden Göttern Dank.

Hast du
jede Erfahrung vergessen:

Gewesensein,
die Lebendigen lieben's

als Gegenstand.

Age-old understanding. For that
thanks to the absent gods.

Have you
forgotten your every experience:

Having-been—
the living love it

as an object.

Die wahrhaft
rand- und

grundlose Schlucht,
Himmel geheißen

(Wort
während deiner Zeit),

birgt nicht Mensch
und nicht Gott.

The truly
edge- and

groundless ravine,
known as heaven

(a word
during your time),

shelters not man
and not God.

Es war Mai,
Juni auch, und es wurde
manches empfunden
betreffs der Natur.

Diese, sich über
den Weltabgrund neigend
mit Gleichmut. O
goldener Ginster.

It was May,
June too, and some
things were felt
regarding nature.

This, leaning over
the abyss of the world
with equanimity. O
golden gorse.

Schön ist
die Erde in sich.
Es gibt

kein Gedächtnis
außerhalb ihrer.
Die Hoffnung

findest du drüben
als der Vorstellung
Leichnam.

In itself,
Earth is beautiful.
There is

no memory
outside of it.
You will find

hope over there,
as representation's
corpse.

Es ist,
Staub zu sein,
wirklich kein Amt.

O
Öde immerdar,
der Ewigkeit Wüste.

Geboren,
bin ich
ins Wissen geworfen.

To be
dust isn't really
an official function.

O
only desolation,
eternity's desert.

Once born,
I was
flung into knowledge.

Frag dich dereinst
(du kannst es nicht),
mit hohlem Schädel frag's:

»Die Sorgen aus dem Geiste«—
was

meinte Hölderlin damit?

Ask yourself someday
(you can't do it),
with hollow skull ask it:

"The cares out of the mind"—
what

did Hölderlin mean by that?

Du sagst, es sei
das Einzige, dieses
Hier, und das
ist wahr, gewiß.

Doch nehmen sich
wenige wirklich
des Atems an.
Die meisten suchen

das Denken nicht,
und viele
sind gefangen
in Not.

You say, it is
the only thing, this
Here, and that
is true, for sure.

But only a few
actually attend
to breathing.
Most do not seek

thinking,
and many
are snared
in distress.

Sei, Erde, gesegnet
mit meiner Mutter
Knochen und meines Vaters
Verwestheit. Ich folge.

Ach, war ich nicht sie
und erzeugte mich,
zu erblicken
die Erscheinungen?

Be blessed, Earth,
with my mother's
bones and my father's
decayedness. I'm to follow.

Ah, was I not they,
and did I not engender me
to lay eyes on
these apparitions?

Der Erkennende
ist der Gräber,
die Erkenntnis das

Grab. Der
Gipfel der Ohnmacht
ist unten.

The one who understands
is the digger,
understanding the

grave. The
peak of powerlessness
is down there.

(In den beiden folgenden Gedichten wird aus
Bobrowskis »Epilog auf Hamann« zitiert.)

Zum Leben
verhält sich
Leben, nichts

außerdem. Das
Andere
ist »dort, wo man

nichts
nichts
nichts gedenkt«,

auf ewig.

(In both of the following poems, Bobrowski's
"Epilogue to Hamann" is quoted.)

Life
relates to
living, nothing

more. The
other
is "there, where one

remembers nothing
nothing
nothing,"

eternally.

Der Erde Eigenes
sind die Früchte,
und die Luft ist es
in den Höhlen.

Honig aß ich,
»taumelnd vom Geruch
meiner eigenen
Verwesung«.

What is Earth's own
are the fruits,
and in caverns
it is the air.

I ate honey,
"reeling from the smell
of my own
decay."

Es schreit
eine Stimme.
Diese

ist wessen?
Gelassen
geht einer,

weil alles
ihm fremd Geschickte
in Wahrheit

sein Eigentum ist.

A voice
is screaming.
This

is whose?
Someone walks
serenely,

because all that's sent
him from parts unknown
is in truth

his own property.

Vor meinen Augen
breitet sich
HADES. O

Name. Endlich,
wenn du dich auflöst
in Todesschweiß,

wird alles
getaucht ins
Wahre.

Before my eyes
is spread out
HADES. O

name. When
you finally dissolve
in the sweat of death,

everything
will be plunged
into truth.

Spät in der Zeit
wirst du sagen,
du seist

ein Mensch gewesen.

Du sagst es nicht,
kannst es nicht sagen—
du sagst es jetzt.

Late in time
you will say
that you

were once a person.

You don't say it,
cannot say it—
you say it now.

OUR WORK ON THIS TRANSLATION WAS PARTLY
FUNDED BY THE UNIVERSITY OF DENVER AND
THE PENNSYLVANIA STATE UNIVERSITY. WE WISH
TO THANK LEA PAO FOR HER THOUGHTFUL FEED-
BACK, AND ESPECIALLY STEPHANIE JORDANS
AND DOMINIK LOOGEN AT THE ERNST MEISTER
ARBEITSSTELLE IN AACHEN FOR WELCOMING
US AND DEEPENING OUR UNDERSTANDING OF
MEISTER AND HIS POETRY.